Scooters

Quinn M. Arnold

seedlings

CREATIVE EDUCATION • CREATIVE PAPERBACKS

Published by Creative Education and Creative Paperbacks
P.O. Box 227, Mankato, Minnesota 56002
Creative Education and Creative Paperbacks
are imprints of The Creative Company
www.thecreativecompany.us

Design by Ellen Huber; production by Mary Herrmann
Art direction by Rita Marshall
Printed in the United States of America

Photographs by Alamy (kevin cable), BigStock (Evgenyjs1),
Dreamstime (Valuavitaly), Getty Images (Aaron Foster/The Image
Bank, Kyle Krause/Photolibrary, Inti St Clair, Granger Wootz/Blend
Images), iStockphoto (CraigRJD, HKPNC, leezsnow, Meinzahn,
MichaelSvoboda, selimaksan, Evgeniy Skripnichenko, tataks),
Shutterstock (FamVeld, GOLFX, Here, PRESSLAB, Romrodphoto,
Ljupco Smokovski, zhukovvvlad)

Library of Congress Cataloging-in-Publication Data
Names: Arnold, Quinn M., author.
Title: Scooters / Quinn M. Arnold.
Series: Seedlings.
Includes index.
Summary: A kindergarten-level introduction to the vehicles
known as scooters, covering their purpose, parts, and operation,
and such defining features as their decks and brakes.
Identifiers: LCCN 2018053210 / ISBN 978-1-64026-171-6
(hardcover) / ISBN 978-1-62832-734-2 (pbk) /
ISBN 978-1-64000-289-0 (eBook)

Subjects: LCSH: Scooters—Juvenile literature. / Scootering—
Juvenile literature.
Classification: LCC GV859.77.A76 2019 / DDC 796.7/5—dc23

CCSS: RI.K.1, 2, 3, 4, 5, 6, 7; RI.1.1, 2, 3, 4, 5, 6, 7;
RF.K.1, 3; RF.1.1

First Edition HC 9 8 7 6 5 4 3 2 1
First Edition PBK 9 8 7 6 5 4 3 2 1

TABLE OF CONTENTS

Time to go!

Scooters are used outside.

They travel on roads.

They roll down sidewalks.

Two wheels turn
under the deck.
The handlebar
stem is tall.

Handlebars steer the front wheel.

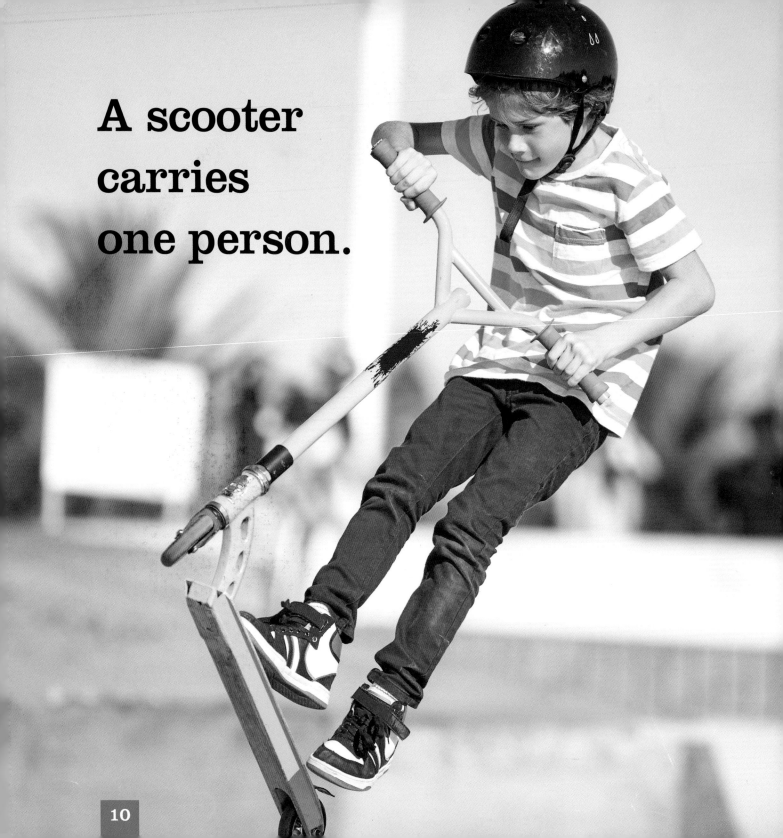

A scooter
carries
one person.

The rider stands on the deck.

One foot is in front of the other.

Batteries power electric scooters. Push scooters are powered by the rider.

All riders should wear helmets.

The rider pushes
off the ground. This
starts the scooter.

A brake slows it down.

brake

A scooter races along a smooth path.

It slows down to turn a corner.

Go, scooter, go!

push scooter

handlebar

handlebar stem

brake

deck

wheel

kickstand

20

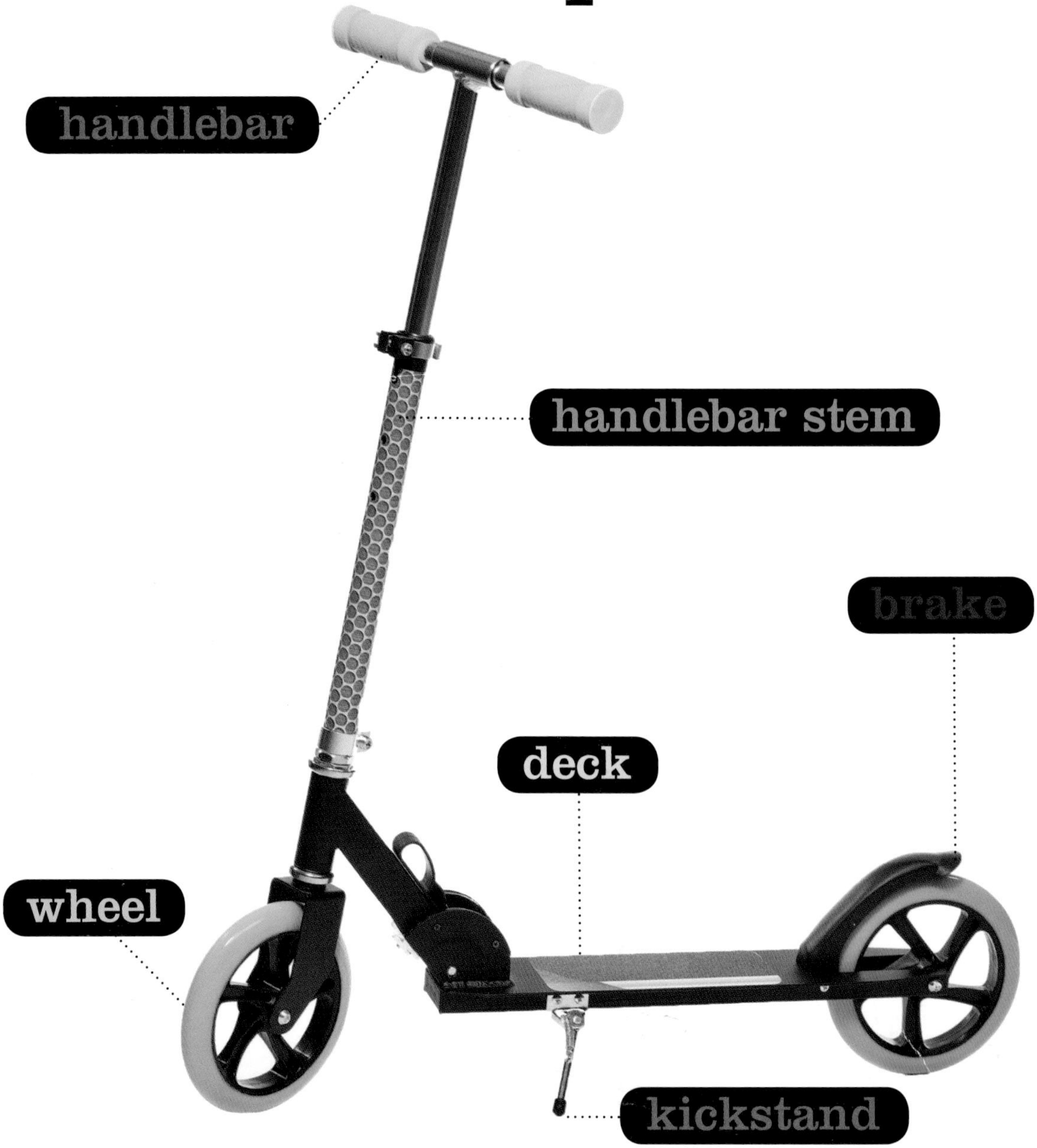

throttle

electric scooter

handlebar

brake lever

brake line

handlebar stem

deck

wheel

kickstand

Words to Know

batteries: containers in which energy is made into electricity to provide power

deck: the part of the scooter that a rider stands on

steer: to turn or guide the movement of a vehicle

Read More

Blaine, Victor. *My Scooter*.
New York: PowerKids Press, 2015.

Peyton, Katherine. *Ripsticks and Scooters*.
New York: Cavendish Square, 2014.

Websites

Printable Coloring Pages: Push Scooter
https://printablefreecoloring.com/drawings/transportation
/push-scooter/
Print out pictures of scooters to color.

YouTube: 5 Beginner Scooter Tricks
https://www.youtube.com/watch?v=lx9taykRJ2c
Learn how to do easy tricks on a scooter!

Index